Tips for Using This Prayer

Engaging in meaningful conversation and spending quality time with a friend or loved one is the foundation upon which we build our relationships. Likewise, those same dynamics are also the foundation upon which we build a relationship with God, as that's essentially what prayer is: quality time and quality communication with God. Both speaking to God, as well as listening to God. Just as we communicate with friends and loved ones in many ways, there are also many different ways that we can communicate with God through prayer, as prayer comes in a wide variety of styles and methods.

No matter if it's praying with the Bible or other Sacred texts, reading a soul-stirring spiritual book, praising God in song, reciting time-honored traditional prayers, or simply talking to God in one's own words, God speaks to us in many different ways and is present at every moment of our lives. Thus, the heart of prayer is an ever-growing awareness of God's presence and a continual raising of our mind and heart to God throughout each day. In this sense, our entire life can be an ongoing prayer and we truly begin to "pray unceasingly" as St. Paul recommended in 1 Thessalonians 5:16-18.

It's truly amazing how God interacts with us in our daily lives. Sometimes He is unmistakably, powerfully present to us, and at other times He whispers His wisdom to us in the silence of our hearts. Sometimes God speaks to us through the words of a complete stranger or strengthens and sanctifies us by means of the hardships we endure on the journey of life. Whatever the case may be, take confidence in the fact that God is with you at all times and that He loves you far greater than you can possibly imagine!

The pages of this journal are intended to record the highlights of your journey with the Lord. They can be used to document your interactions with God, whether they be big or small, life-changing or casual. They can be used to make note of the inspiration you receive, to count your blessings, or to track your progress while working through a difficult time. Use these pages however you see fit and revisit them often, especially in times of darkness and doubt. For indeed, His amazing grace will always lead you to the light.

About the Divine Mercy Image

The image featured on the cover of this journal is that of the Divine Mercy of Jesus. For four years, starting in 1931, Jesus appeared to a young Polish nun named Sister Faustina Kowalska. He appeared to her as the now-famous painting depicts, in a white garment with red and pale rays coming forth from His Sacred Heart, and His hand extending a blessing.

Jesus gave a special mission to Sister (now Saint) Faustina. He instructed her, "I am sending you with My mercy to the people of the whole world. I do not want to punish mankind, but I desire to heal it, pressing it to My merciful Heart." He also revealed to her, "You are the secretary of My Mercy. I have chosen you for that office in this and the next life."

One particular way to spread the message of Jesus' mercy was by means of the Divine Mercy Image. As Jesus said to Saint Faustina, "Paint an image according to the pattern you see, with the signature: Jesus, I trust in You. I promise that the soul that will venerate this image will not perish. I also promise victory over one's enemies already here on earth, especially at the hour of death." Along with the prayerful veneration of the Divine Mercy image, Jesus also taught Sister Faustina powerful prayers to share with the world, such as the *Chaplet of Divine Mercy* and the *Divine Mercy Novena*. He also requested that a *Feast of Divine Mercy* be established which is now celebrated on the Sunday after Easter. Finally, Sister Faustina wrote a diary that records all the details of her many visions of Jesus and the messages He gave her. This diary has been made into a very popular book and is available in stores all over the world.

OUR Father, who art
in heaven, Hallowed be
thy name.
Thy will be done on earth as
it is in heaven.
Give us this day our daily
Bread, and Forgive us our
Trespasses, as we Forgive
those who Trespass against
us, and lead us not into
Temptation, But deliver us
From Evil AMEN

DATE_____

_____

_____

_____

_____

_____

_____

_____

_____

_____

_____

_____

_____

_____

_____

_____

_____

_____

_____

_____

_____

_____

_____

_____

_____

_____

DATE_____

DATE_____

DATE_____

_____

_____

_____

_____

_____

_____

_____

_____

_____

_____

_____

_____

_____

_____

_____

_____

_____

_____

_____

_____

_____

_____

_____

_____

_____

_____

_____

_____

DATE_____

DATE_____

DATE_____

DATE_____

_____
_____
_____
_____
_____
_____
_____
_____
_____
_____
_____
_____
_____
_____
_____
_____
_____
_____
_____
_____
_____
_____
_____
_____
_____
_____
_____
_____
_____

DATE_____

DATE_____

_____
_____
_____
_____
_____
_____
_____
_____
_____
_____
_____
_____
_____
_____
_____
_____
_____
_____
_____
_____
_____
_____
_____
_____
_____
_____
_____
_____
_____

DATE_____

_____
_____
_____
_____
_____
_____
_____
_____
_____
_____
_____
_____
_____
_____
_____
_____
_____
_____
_____
_____
_____
_____
_____
_____
_____
_____
_____
_____
_____
_____
_____
_____

DATE_____

_____

_____

_____

_____

_____

_____

_____

_____

_____

_____

_____

_____

_____

_____

_____

_____

_____

_____

_____

_____

_____

_____

_____

_____

DATE_____

DATE_____

_____
_____
_____
_____
_____
_____
_____
_____
_____
_____
_____
_____
_____
_____
_____
_____
_____
_____
_____
_____
_____
_____
_____
_____
_____
_____

DATE_____

_____
_____
_____
_____
_____
_____
_____
_____
_____
_____
_____
_____
_____
_____
_____
_____
_____
_____
_____
_____
_____
_____
_____
_____
_____
_____
_____

DATE_____

DATE_____

DATE_____

_____

_____

_____

_____

_____

_____

_____

_____

_____

_____

_____

_____

_____

_____

_____

_____

_____

_____

_____

_____

_____

_____

_____

_____

_____

_____

_____

_____

_____

DATE_____

DATE_____

_____
_____
_____
_____
_____
_____
_____
_____
_____
_____
_____
_____
_____
_____
_____
_____
_____
_____
_____
_____
_____
_____
_____
_____
_____
_____
_____
_____

DATE_____

DATE_____

DATE_____

DATE_____

DATE_____

DATE_____

DATE_____

DATE_____

DATE_____

DATE_____

DATE_____

DATE_____

DATE_____

_____
_____
_____
_____
_____
_____
_____
_____
_____
_____
_____
_____
_____
_____
_____
_____
_____
_____
_____
_____
_____
_____
_____
_____
_____

DATE_____

DATE_____

_____
_____
_____
_____
_____
_____
_____
_____
_____
_____
_____
_____
_____
_____
_____
_____
_____
_____
_____
_____
_____
_____
_____
_____
_____
_____
_____
_____

DATE_____

_____

_____

_____

_____

_____

_____

_____

_____

_____

_____

_____

_____

_____

_____

_____

_____

_____

_____

_____

_____

_____

_____

_____

_____

_____

_____

DATE_____

DATE_____

DATE_____

DATE_____

DATE_____

DATE_____

DATE_____

DATE_____

DATE_____

DATE_____

_____

_____

_____

_____

_____

_____

_____

_____

_____

_____

_____

_____

_____

_____

_____

_____

_____

_____

_____

_____

_____

_____

_____

_____

_____

_____

_____

_____

DATE_____

DATE_____

DATE_____

DATE_____

DATE_____

_____

_____

_____

_____

_____

_____

_____

_____

_____

_____

_____

_____

_____

_____

_____

_____

_____

_____

_____

_____

_____

_____

_____

_____

_____

_____

_____

_____

DATE_____

_____
_____
_____
_____
_____
_____
_____
_____
_____
_____
_____
_____
_____
_____
_____
_____
_____
_____
_____
_____
_____
_____
_____
_____

DATE_____

DATE_____

_____
_____
_____
_____
_____
_____
_____
_____
_____
_____
_____
_____
_____
_____
_____
_____
_____
_____
_____
_____
_____
_____
_____
_____
_____
_____
_____
_____
_____
_____

DATE_____

DATE_____

_____

_____

_____

_____

_____

_____

_____

_____

_____

_____

_____

_____

_____

_____

_____

_____

_____

_____

_____

_____

_____

_____

_____

_____

_____

_____

DATE_____

DATE_____

DATE_____

DATE_____

DATE_____

_____

_____

_____

_____

_____

_____

_____

_____

_____

_____

_____

_____

_____

_____

_____

_____

_____

_____

_____

_____

_____

_____

_____

_____

_____

_____

_____

DATE_____

DATE_____

DATE_____

_____
_____
_____
_____
_____
_____
_____
_____
_____
_____
_____
_____
_____
_____
_____
_____
_____
_____
_____
_____
_____
_____
_____
_____
_____
_____
_____

DATE_____

DATE_____

_____

_____

_____

_____

_____

_____

_____

_____

_____

_____

_____

_____

_____

_____

_____

_____

_____

_____

_____

_____

_____

_____

_____

_____

_____

_____

_____

DATE_____

DATE_____

DATE_____

DATE_____

_____
_____
_____
_____
_____
_____
_____
_____
_____
_____
_____
_____
_____
_____
_____
_____
_____
_____
_____
_____
_____
_____
_____
_____
_____
_____
_____
_____

DATE_____

DATE_____

DATE_____

_____

_____

_____

_____

_____

_____

_____

_____

_____

_____

_____

_____

_____

_____

_____

_____

_____

_____

_____

_____

_____

_____

_____

_____

_____

_____

_____

DATE_____

DATE_____

DATE_____

DATE_____

DATE_____

DATE_____

DATE_____

DATE_____

DATE_____

DATE_____

DATE_____

DATE_____

DATE_____

DATE_____

DATE_____

DATE_____

DATE_____

_____

_____

_____

_____

_____

_____

_____

_____

_____

_____

_____

_____

_____

_____

_____

_____

_____

_____

_____

_____

_____

_____

_____

_____

_____

_____

_____

_____

DATE_____

DATE_____

DATE_____

DATE_____

DATE_____

DATE_____

DATE_____

DATE_____

DATE_____

DATE_____

DATE_____

DATE_____

DATE_____

DATE_____

DATE_____

DATE_____

DATE_____

DATE_____

DATE_____

DATE_____

DATE_____

DATE_____

DATE_____

DATE_____

DATE_____

DATE_____

DATE_____

DATE_____

_____
_____
_____
_____
_____
_____
_____
_____
_____
_____
_____
_____
_____
_____
_____
_____
_____
_____
_____
_____
_____
_____
_____
_____
_____
_____
_____
_____
_____

DATE_____

DATE＿＿＿＿＿＿＿＿＿＿＿＿＿＿＿＿＿＿＿

DATE_____

DATE_____

DATE_____

DATE_____

DATE_____

DATE_____

DATE_____

DATE_____

DATE_____

DATE_____

_____

_____

_____

_____

_____

_____

_____

_____

_____

_____

_____

_____

_____

_____

_____

_____

_____

_____

_____

_____

_____

_____

_____

_____

_____

_____

_____

DATE_____

DATE_____

DATE_____

DATE_____

DATE_____

DATE_____

DATE_____

DATE_____

_____

_____

_____

_____

_____

_____

_____

_____

_____

_____

_____

_____

_____

_____

_____

_____

_____

_____

_____

_____

_____

_____

_____

_____

_____

_____

_____

DATE_____

DATE_____

_____
_____
_____
_____
_____
_____
_____
_____
_____
_____
_____
_____
_____
_____
_____
_____
_____
_____
_____
_____
_____
_____
_____
_____
_____

DATE_____

DATE_____

DATE_____

DATE_____

DATE_____

DATE_____

DATE_____

DATE_____

DATE_____

DATE_____

DATE_____

DATE_____

DATE_____

Build Your Prayer Journal Library

**Order additional copies
at
Amazon.com or Prayerwarriorpress.com**

PRAYER WARRIOR PRESS

Prayer Warrior Press produces a wide variety of inspirational, educational, and practical Christian books and gifts.

Visit us today at www.prayerwarriorpress.com

Thank You!

Thank you for purchasing this book. We are extremely grateful. If you enjoyed this book, we'd like to hear from you and hope that you could take some time to post an honest review on Amazon. Your feedback and support will help *Prayer Warrior Press* improve the quality of our products for the future.

Printed in Great Britain
by Amazon